Moments

Linda Collins Thomas

Magical Moments
Copyright © 2024 Linda Collins Thomas

Visit our website at
www.StillwaterPress.com
for more information.

First Stillwater River Publications Edition.

ISBN: 978-1-963296-82-2

1 2 3 4 5 6 7 8 9 10
Written by Linda Collins Thomas.
Cover & interior book design by Matthew St. Jean.
Photograph of Carnegie Hall by
Ajay Suresh / Wikimedia Commons.
Photograph of Gloria Steinem by
Gage Skidmore / Wikimedia Commons.
Published by Stillwater River Publications,
West Warwick, RI, USA.

and
Honey the Cat

Their love makes our house a home.

And

Ben, David and Andrew Thomas

My sons, my heart, my laughter, my joy.

Acknowledgments

My first thank you is to Samantha Clark, URI graduate from the Cyber-Senior Program at the Osher Lifelong Learning Institute. She was my cyber-buddy and we met weekly at a local coffee house where she showed me how to place my diaries and writings on my own website. Because of the OLLI program and Samantha's skill and friendship, I discovered that you can leap forward even in senior years and increase your public contribution and probably add years to your life!

I have additional gratitude in discovering Steve and Dawn Porter of Stillwater Press, owners of the Stillwater Book Store in West Warwick. Their new location is also the residence of Freddie the cat. It was great to meet another literary cat, since I have one too. I learned the process of getting my website essays published. I can't thank them enough for their exceptional professionalism, their encouragement and their guidance, while of-

My last thank you as this goes to press is a big thank you to all the friends, family, and teachers who gave me courage to know I would be a published writer someday. I'm so glad I didn't wait a minute longer.

Contents

A Cabin in the Forest

As an experiment in connecting with my son's lifestyle and values, I traveled to Alaska in 1991 and lived for two awe-inspiring cabin-in-the wilderness-weeks in Findlay Forest, Fairbanks, Alaska, where Ben was attending the University of Alaska Fairbanks. He and Julie had just gotten engaged and were living in Findlay Forest. Luck was clearly on my path when Ben's friend, Emeritus Gordon Wright,

founder of the Fairbanks Symphony Orchestra, graciously offered his hand-built cabin for my stay, as he was spending the summer in Anchorage.

Gordon had furnished his beautiful cabin with all the comforts of home, while maintaining a sustenance life style. The front door had the standard rope pull which allowed the door to open only outward. A hand carved sign warmly announced, "Welcome Weary Travelers." Inside, a sleeping loft with a ladder (to be hauled upward after retiring) was a further security option against hungry four legged forest intruders. Propane gas sup-

tery that allowed for music to play a fabulous collection of classical symphonic tapes that soothed the heart and stirred the life – that came from the house that Gordon built. And, I might add, reverberated through the forest for the foxes and chatty red squirrels to enjoy.

Cold butter, milk and meat and beer were stored in a well-dug hole in the earth outdoors that descended into very cold permafrost. Indoors, a wood stove provided meals, hot coffee and general warmth when needed. Water was transported from town and used for drinking. Rain barrel water was collected and was used for dishes and a good body splash when going to the University showers was not a necessity. A fully operational hand built sauna was a few feet from the house, completely private and peaceful. And yes, a fully equipped outhouse was part of life in the forest. Mr. Wright's cabin home was filled with literature and art work of the Alaskan heart. His dwelling was well crafted and secure, designed in harmony with nature. I particularly remember his many pairs of large boots and work shoes, neatly lined up inside the door, under the wooden pegs for heavy jackets and shirts, when coming and going.

Ben lent me his dog, a happy Labrador, for companionship. Salsa accompanied me on walks along the

trails of Findlay Forest until we circled back, Ben's forest map in hand, or until we got to my car in a communal parking area one half mile away.

I had no cell phone, no laptop in that year. I learned to live by my wits and inclinations. Each day only required knowing how to provide for the basics of building a fire, putting the kettle on, greeting the morning on the porch, getting nourishment, using water consciously, and living in connection with what was available in nature.

I kept a journal of my thoughts and my activities and I still reread it when I long to return to feelings of simplicity and beauty. I was a car drive away from groceries, ice cream parlor, and hardware stores. But I stayed secluded and happy, except for evening visits with Ben

berry and raspberry cobbler for dessert, along with out-door fire, guitar music, happy dogs, and Alaska news updates. My visit coincided with the fantastic Alaska Folk Festival, where people gathered on the grass and could get a sun tan as late as 8 p.m. while picnicking, singing, and getting their groove on.

Magical memories are my walks through the wood chip trails of this forest. I took along Salsa for compa-ny and safety and a soup can of pebbles to rattle. That was the local (Ben's) advice to alert shy bears with poor vision that a human was in the area where berry bush-es might be too engrossing. I don't remember being frightened at all. My second day is when the miracle started happening. A snowy white owl, who is usually a night owl, began guiding me along the trail. He would

tire stay. He had an immense wing span and a beautifully feathered white body. Perhaps he was considering me to be a small mouse. Nevertheless, he was my constant reminder of the mystery.

A word about forest fragrances. Beside the fresh air that cleansed everything in sight twenty-four hours every day, bringing unimaginable goodness into my lungs, there is the smell of cedar, especially after the rain. The crunch of spruce needles underfoot that release a citrusy delight. I understand that bears have an intense sense of smell and I think humans have a similar brain pathway to awaken them, if only we take the time.

When I was packing to leave and Ben and Julie were transporting me to the airport. Julie said, "Did you tell your mom about the bear break-in?" Ben quickly said, "Shhh. I didn't." I asked, "What bear break-in?" Then they revealed that the week-before I'd arrived, a bear had found its way inside one of the nearby cabins that was vacant and ransacked it pretty good.

Gordon Wright died in 2007 and his obituary was in the New York Times. I can't say thank you ever, ever enough to this lovely man for his generosity. I learned in those two weeks what matters in the art of daily living. I applaud others who are determined to keep a

I highly recommend you take an unforgettable trip to the forest! The smells. The sunlight dappling the earth beneath your soft footfalls. The music of the trees. The peace that passeth all understanding. It also might be a good idea to pack a can of pebbles.

How many women out there have seen "Educating Rita," either the 1983 film or the current staged production at 2nd Story Theatre in Warren, Rhode Island? And did you relate to Rita?

Rita White spoke for a whole generation of women when she was penned by Willy Russell. I personally loved the line, "I want to sing me own song," when Rita found herself gob-smacked between two worlds. There was the known world of her hair salon, of extended family providing a sense of belonging and certainty as they sang together at the local pub; the other, the unknown but extraordinarily exciting world of academic learning when going to University for the first time. Not knowing what she got herself in for, but knowing that it made her heart race with excitement, Rita hung in for the ride of her life. For me, as for Rita, it was exactly like discovering diamonds and gold that nobody ever told you were yours for the taking. Rita simply wanted, in her words,

I was Rita, beginning around 1975, married with three children. But the awakening can occur at any age. It most often follows a newly intruding restlessness while not knowing what is happening in your secure, unquestioned life. Gloria Steinem called it, *The Revolution Within*. I encourage women to welcome it. Consider yourself one of the lucky ones. Many people live an entire lifetime without ever waking up and the universe has chosen YOU to find your purpose. How cool is that?

Not that this strange upsetting of the apple cart isn't without turmoil and consequence. You might find yourself needing to get acquainted with your inner warrior. In fact, it's recommended.

Be prepared to take a stand.

I was told we couldn't afford my little hobby of taking classes. I was also told by people who mattered that I was being selfish to my family just to satisfy a whim. My neighbor told me her husband wants his dinner on the table when he gets home. No, that would never work, she said emphatically. And studying at night after getting the kids to bed? No thanks! I looked next to my educated (PhD) friend whom I'd met in childbirth classes and who valued higher learning above all, but she want-

There you have it. This is what you may have deal with: dismissal, minimizing your new found excitement, pointing out why it won't work, outright jealousy, people not wanting you to change, people thinking you've gone off the deep end and perhaps your mom saying, as mine did, "Do you know how *old* you will be before you even have a degree, much less a job?" So I learned to say, "I'm going to be that old anyway, so I want to have something to show for it when I get there." Then, be prepared to hear that you are not the nice person they once knew and they don't know what's gotten into you.

Be prepared to feel stung.

The whim comment stung the most. A whim is a capricious impulse. That is why one refers to the whimsical as cute and not to be taken too seriously. This passionate pull on me was the very opposite of a whim. This was my soul calling out to me. No kidding.

Be prepared to have your own doubts.

My baby sitter did her homework at our house – algebra, trigonometry, and such. Good grief, I never did that in high school and now I thought I could go to college? I had those awful dreams where I was asked to stand up in class, after being late because I couldn't

Be prepared for a change in relationships.

I didn't know that my husband was not on board when I announced with pleasure that I wanted to take some classes. That was another dawning to be added to the soup. I thought he would be happy, maybe even proud. He went to college, but that was different, he said. He went at the right time, after high school, before marriage and family were created. His parents agreed. He did the right thing. He was the provider and he would always take care of me. It is true. He always seemed to be looking after my welfare bringing home surprises like a brand new TV, a new washing machine, even a new car. He did the shopping for the big price items. I named the children. But apparently my getting a college degree was over the top of what a wife should think about, let alone send for a catalog and actually sign up for a class. How could I do that to him? It would take me away from hearth and home and maybe even put "ideas" in my head, I was duly warned.

Be prepared to persevere.

There are lighter moments too. My mother worried that "the hippies" got a hold of me at college and "gave me some of their pot".

So, be prepared to overlook any implication that

keep on believing because that same mother of mine called later, much later, after I had graduated with two degrees and opened a practice, after seven years learning much at a mental health agency. She said, "Linda, I want to buy the sign for your new office and one for your front door. I'm so proud of you. I have to admit, you did it entirely on your own, with no support from me. I don't know how you did it." I said, "Thank you, that means a lot to me." Then I brushed myself off and went shopping for a sign maker and sent her a picture when I hung it. So, there you are. Sometimes it takes a while.

I was fortified by Gloria Steinem's essay, "Ruth's Song Because She Couldn't Sing It." Ruth, of course, was her mother. Sometimes, we daughters have to take the bull by the horns and refuse to settle, knowing that we are moving forward for both ourselves *and* our mothers.

And I did have my angels. I'll never forget Mr. William Temple, librarian at a community college where I began with my toe in the water. One day, checking out my books, he said to me, "This place is not the best for you, Linda. Conn College offers a Return to College Program and they have a great faculty there. I think you will find yourself thriving there."

a no nonsense bustling woman of years, with the college since its days of Connecticut College for Women. She hustled me over to meet with Department Chairs to whom she would say, "This woman is going somewhere" as I thought, "Really?" while the Rita in me thought, "I just want to sing me own song." Dean Johnson gave me stern guidance as well as unending support and genuine affection.

And a moment of profound gratitude here is called for to my instructors and professors who took a serious interest in my papers and gave me advice in a way that said, "I believe in you."

I discovered friendships with other older woman students in different majors, along with bright and lively young students, who paved the way for me to connect to learning as an intellectual adventure, not only the means to a job.

One of my best friends was Katherine, single with a young child. She studied mathematics, then majored in chemistry, then went on to become a med student at UPenn and today she's a doctor in Boston. She had come to this country from Greece with her parents, had a marriage arranged for her, realized she had a mind for learning, and got brave enough to strike out on her

own. When that happened her father had a heart attack. But she didn't quit her dreams and hard work. She was a Rita too.

In sharing some of my story, I hope you will find courage to always count on your own inner light to be your guide. And teachers will appear at the right time, along with rewards you never dreamed possible.

Growing Up at Funerals

Sometimes even an optimist has to write about her sadness.

When you are four years old, you and your twin brother, Lance, attend your first funeral. It is a fascinating event. Your mother keeps pulling you and Lance out from the folds of dark red velvet curtains that you've been hiding in. People are smiling, even winking, at you. Grandpa Longe died. You don't know what that means. I think it means we have to behave while the grownups talk in somber tones for a long time. Grandpa would not like that. Grandpa liked to laugh. Where was Grandpa? A poke comes from the curtains. You enter the soft wonderful world of red velvet again to find Lance – until your mother takes you firmly by the hand and says you and brother are going to have sandwiches and cake. This is fun. Why is Grandma crying? I will give her some of my cake.

When you are seventeen, you and Lance are sitting in the front row of chairs at Barley's Funeral Home in

pers," If you aren't going up, then I'm not either." You love him for that. Uncle Ralph went and had a fit when he read Grandma's final wishes on a nice piece of linen note paper she had carefully folded in her underwear and handkerchief drawer. She asked for a closed casket. That's all she wanted. Grandma was a proud woman. She was never without her nylon stockings, fresh handkerchiefs scented with White Shoulders perfume and a touch of blue rinse in her white hair. She didn't want anyone to see her dead. You understand that. Why can't Uncle Ralph? All your aunts, including your mother, remain silent about it. What's *wrong* with them, you wonder? Are they going to sit there crying and let Uncle Ralph call all the shots? Where are people's morals these days? Where is their devotion to their mother? You are so frustrated you could cry, but you promised Grandma you wouldn't cry at her funeral. Instead you think of the quilt she made for you as you fight back a flood of tears along with a monumental desire to tell off Uncle Ralph.

Daddy's funeral came out the blue. Sixty-nine years old and handsome as ever. Mother is angry. She said it was the cigarettes. If he cared about us, he would have stopped, she said. You and Lance talk over how to sup-

talk her out of that idea by reminding her he never took it off once in forty-four years. You hear her mention it again at the grave site, coming in over the minister's voice, causing him to lose his place in the liturgy. Lance takes your hand. You both exchange glances and try very hard not to break the silence through lips drawn tight, eyes down, in an effort to not let any wrong sound escape.

Twenty-one years later, her hands are folded in a supposed kind of peaceful acceptance, but you know it wasn't true. Your breath sears your lungs sharply as it occurs to you that these are the same hands that once guided you out mischief and toward nourishment and good manners when you were four years old. You are overwhelmed with sadness, but comforted by Lance who is your rock, your friend, or as he calls you, "My favorite womb-mate." You and Lance are the constant thread in this fabric of family cloth. Now it is up to you to weave the next length. All you have are your memories, the present moment, and each other.

Lance's funeral. Where to begin? Wait, this is not supposed to happen. My buddy, my brother, is supposed to be sitting here beside me, holding my hand, so we can cry or laugh together. I don't even want to be here. I'm

glancing around for a red velvet curtain where we can play hide and seek and all this will go away. But I only see a shiny casket and I hear soft music and low voices. Please, someone come and get me and take me back to my childhood where cake makes everything better.

Previously published in Amherst Writers & Artists Press, The Peregrine Journal, *2022.*

Old Man Winneger

More often than most of us realize, our futures are set down in early events and experiences that may seem small and ordinary at the time, but are in fact big, even claiming the status of a breakthrough. Today on my son Ben's birthday, such an event stays in my memory from my life as a young, guileless, untested wife and mother. It wasn't until someone important to me declared, several years later, I think you are going to be a therapist, that the ground had already been laid for my career on that one day in the summer of 1972.

I guess every childhood neighborhood has a mean old man. At least ours did. He was "Old Man Winneger." Legend had it that he had been a firefighter in his younger days and then he retired and built a beautiful house for Marty, his sweet

It was the summer of 1972 and my children were nine, six and four years old. Summer evenings were magical times back then. After supper, the boys ran across the meadow of field grasses following a well-trodden path that led from our remodeled farm house to Bluebird Road. Bluebird Road was ideally named. A secluded wooded area of homes that had sprung up in our beautiful shoreline town in Connecticut.

There they played hide and seek and Red Rover with the neighborhood kids until mothers called them inside. About eight o'clock, I crossed the meadow in the dusky light and retrieved them for their bedtime. It was a ritual of bubbly baths, snacks and bedtime stories. Amidst cuddles, laughter and clean sheets that had dried in the sun, my cubs drifted into innocent dreams of safety, their hair still damp on their pillows.

One memorable evening, Ben came bolting across the field about 7 o'clock and breathlessly announced that "Mr. Winneger said he was going to get his gun and shoot Lady!" I dropped my tea towel and grabbed Ben's hand.

We crossed to Bluebird Road in seconds. In short order I corralled David and Andrew who were standing in the road wide-eyed, holding onto our docile aging

then returned to the kitchen to ponder what I should do next.

I was a shy, young homemaker and had never encountered anyone who owned a gun, much less scared young children by threatening to shoot their dog. I took a very deep breath, straightened my shoulders as my grandmother had done in times of uncertainty. I decided right then and there that I had to give Mr. Winneger, a man I'd never met, a good talking to.

I marched from the house and never blinked until I reached the front lawn of the Winneger's. The street was quiet. Marty was digging in her flower beds, despite the coming dark. In the dim light, I saw Mr. Winneger on the screened porch, smoking his pipe. Even though the evening was fading I could not allow my courage to fade also. Breathe, I said to myself.

"Bart?" I called.

"What is it!" he growled.

"Bart, it's Linda Thomas from across the field. Lady is our dog. I need to talk." I still had no idea what I was going to say.

At this point, Marty chimed in with her lyrical voice. "Sure, Bart, sure," while motioning him to walk down to the road and greet me.

Ben on his rock with Lady

I reached out my hand and he shook it. I was small, fair, blue-eyed and the opposite of imposing. He was large, craggy, scowling and formidable. I took another deep breath, picturing my kids sleeping back at the house. Or maybe glued to the upstairs windows.

"Bart," I began, "I hear you told my kids you were going to shoot Lady."

"Yeah? Well, she laid down in my wife's tulips."

"Bart, I'm sorry about that, really. I'll try to keep her on her leash. Usually she stays at home. But, see, if this

"My wife has her gardens. She works hard."

I walked over to inspect the damage. It looked like Lady had decided to lie down in the cool dirt. A fair number of tulips were smashed.

"But Bart, that was extreme. If she gets loose I want you to call me and say, I have your dog."

His head jerked up and he squinted, as he studied me.

"Why should I do that?"

I looked right into his guarded eyes and said the only true thing I could think of. "Well, because I'm your neighbor. We're neighbors, Bart."

Marty chimed in, "Sure Bart, that's right."

I turned and walked home in the twilight, reflecting on this odd encounter.

I felt kind of dizzy.

One evening a few nights later, I walked over to Blue-bird Road to collect my brood for their bath time. As I walked past the Winneger's large front lawn , Mr.Win-neger was smoking his pipe and standing alongside Marty who was weeding.

I glanced over and Mr. Winneger took his pipe out of his mouth. He nodded and said, "Evening, Mrs. Thomas.

"Evening Bart. Evening, Marty," I replied.

Shortly after that, I took Marty some fresh tulip bulbs and she accepted them.

Years later, whenever my family gathers for holiday meals, we sometimes tell stories from growing up by Bluebird Road. That's when my grown sons still say, "Mom! Tell us about the time when you straightened out Old Man Winneger!"

What I Learned from Wild Turkeys

*L*iving in the small village of Slocum, Rhode Island, I experience the advantages of quiet evenings. I glance across the road known as "The shortcut to URI" which offers the wide view of picture-perfect sod farms. I wake to refreshing mornings of coffee on the sun porch where I'm surprised by summertime visits from wild turkey families. Yes, wild turkeys have informed my conscious awareness and my happiness in unexpected instances of self-recognition, solace, laughter and peace. Let me count the ways.

My first encounter with this large, shy and yet confident bird family occurred while driving home from my office in Wickford. A line of cars politely and impolitely stopped for a sizeable wild turkey family crossing a back road.

There we all sat in a line next to a fire station and a ball field. One at a time, the turkey family crossed with

music to underscore a theatrical scene. Watching the turkeys, I understood why John Philip Sousa's "Semper Fidelis" was said to bring tears to the composer.

I counted them. Two very large parents with very long necks as leaders, four adolescents on their best behavior, and eight fluffy assorted chicks who looked daunted following them.

I didn't think about the number of cars bound home after a hard day's work. Instead, I experienced one of those helpless moments where reality takesover and we succumb. To tell the truth, this enforced stop was a pleasure. Who knew there might be another way to deepen your breath and find inner peace?

Yes, wild turkeys have informed my conscious awareness and my happiness in unexpected instances of self-recognition, solace, laughter and peace.

The next day, a wild turkey family came to visit our property at dawn. My husband and I had planted a vegetable garden. It was 6 a.m. While making coffee, I passed by the kitchen window and there, in all their quiet confidence, was a very large wild turkey family in the backyard. Trying not to be seen, I observed that the Tom-father bird pecked and pushed the adolescent birds into better choices. They pecked at what may have been bugs

for breakfast along with garden seeds. Momma-Hen attended to the needs of the little chicks. They move elegantly and silently. They lay in the cool soil at the end of the garden and rested. I took another deep breath and rested my mind, which was overrun with chores.

That night, the Tom bird returned to the large roots of our Norwegian Maple tree and taught his male offspring to roost in a tree top for sleep and safety. I did not know turkeys have that ability.

All this to notice they are living courageously in an ecologically dependent system in a world that has become conquering and competitive and not united.

I ponder how we lost our human connection to nature and our means to get along in basic ecology. I feel our future health depends on learning to do this.

One morning, I made a list. I wrote as I looked out the window at the morning visit of the turkeys. "Buy fresh mozzarella for ripe garden tomatoes. Buy Rain Dance for the car windows. Feed the turkeys."

But I didn't feed the turkeys. I came to my senses that I would be interfering with what they already knew how to do.

I looked for information on wild turkeys in Rhode Island and discovered to my delight that my concerns were well covered by our state. The Rhode Island Department of Environmental Management (DEM, annually sends questionnaires out to the public on Reported Sightings of Wild Turkey Broods.

"Today turkeys are found in practically all areas of the state and provide recreational and wildlife viewing opportunities," according to the DEM website.

What I learned from my view out my windows is that wild turkey life involves active interdependency, attachment, mutual agreement for survival and a confident ecology with the planet earth, which is, after all, our only home.

Previously published on RhodeIslandCurrent.com, 2023.

Fear and My Trip to New York

I had my eyes opened yesterday to a wider picture. I've been full of angst about going to New York for a staged reading of David's play, "A Little Lower than the Angels." Reading about heightened security and organized protests, blocked streets, destruction in other cities, I didn't know what to expect in terms of our safety.

Rather than black and white, stay or leave, protest or die, I saw a New York that was just simply beautiful. We traveled to the upper West Side, and spent much of our time between upper Broadway, Columbus and Amsterdam, on 100th, along the very edge of Central Park West. The day was a riot of color and bright sunshine. Families were everywhere, Kids in strollers, on foot, in arms. I never saw so many happy kids as in this lively neighborhood.

Whole Foods was serving an international banquet

performance of Dave's play at the Bloomingdale Branch of the New York Public Library by Break A Leg Productions, we gathered at the Metro Diner at the corner of Broadway and 100th, a not to be missed adventure (I had my first cup of Matzo Ball Soup), a thoroughly New York fresh, big and friendly eating experience.

I cherish the activism that has been a hallmark of our democracy and I will always take part in it. That is not my concern here. I was more concerned that we will allow our fears to paralyze us and keep us from going about living our lives, that is, living in the power of our belief in creating a positive outcome. Yesterday in New York City, I became more than my fears.

My trip to New York was just what I needed to feel like a part of an ocean of diversity and beauty. I was flowing in and part and parcel of why we are together. Here. On Earth. It was a glorious day of theater, food, and meaningful connection to something really, really big.

p.s. David's play was a big hit!!

The Closest I'll Ever Get
to Carnegie Hall

You never know what will develop from a writing prompt until you do it. One must stop when the ding goes off, probably five minutes. The idea is to not correct anything and to practice flowing like a river.

Seen up close, her hair, . . . which sat atop her head like a crown, was the perfect touch. It was a pile of auburn curls that had the comical tendency to slide to the left when she played Verdi, of all things.

Her old world apartment, located across from Carnegie Hall, was filled with framed posters and pictures from dozens of past performances as a once beautiful and highly acclaimed coloratura soprano. Gustava Weiss was a name that time had perhaps forgotten? By way of quick glances, I ascertained the posters to be printed in German. They had a faded quality that belied her grand posture at the piano which dominated the room as I hesitantly entered for my first voice lesson.

She sat with a noble dignity and a sense of purpose. The magnificent grand piano, glowing with aged patina, was covered with a well-loved fringed cloth of ivory linen, a crystal bowl of fragrant peonies adorning the top.

"Now!" she proclaimed with gusto and a strong chord, announcing the lesson had begun. "Now, bella ballerina, bella ballerina," as she encouraged me to vocalize up and down

no no! You must listen with utmost care and do not sing from your throat! Reach deeper, sing from your thighs!" She banged out a chord, as if to accent her command and the pile of curls, which obsessed me, slipped to the right.

Later I descended, as if in a dream, by way of a caged lift and emerged into the bright sunlight of the city street below. Through the open window, four floors above, I heard the faint sounds of the keyboard. ♪♫

Just so I know this was not a dream, I retained a taped recording of my lesson. I was visiting a friend in New York City who took me to the voice lesson with this unforgettable person, whose image returned years later when prompted in my writers group to write from the words, "*Seen up close, her hair . . .*"

That prompt could have gone anywhere. The fact that it tapped into the unexpected is the gift that writing brings us. Stories are waiting to be told in all of us. Perhaps you, dear followers, should give it a try and be as surprised as I was by life's magical moments.

Gustava Weiss died in 2001, at the age of 91.

Marriage Therapy at the Newport Creamery

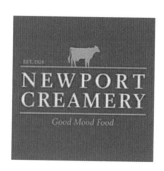

When Christmas shopping with my mother, she used to love to go the Newport Creamery. So today I stopped by for her favorite lunch. Chicken quesadilla. Soon an elderly couple shuffled rather painfully into the booth in front of mine. My thoughts were that I was happy they could be together for Christmas. Then, this conversation:

> She: I'll sit by the window, Daddy, so you won't bitch about the cold air.
>
> He: I don't bitch.
>
> She: Yes you do. You always bitch.

bring your antacids?

He: I don't need my antacids.

She: Yes, you need your antacids. I'm not going to hear it later that you can't sleep from your heartburn.

He: It's your cooking that gives me the heartburn. This here food is made good.

Waitress: Hi folks. Are you ready?

He: Well, Hello sweetheart! Merry Christmas! How are those blueberry muffins today?

She: You can't have those.

Waitress: So nice how your missus looks out for you Frank. I have poached eggs and fruit with your name on it today.

He: That's the ticket sweetheart. Bring me the Frank special. With your smile. And some homefries.

I hope Frank and his wife have a Merry Christmas. God bless waitresses everywhere.

My quesadilla was delicious.

Life is a mystery. Savor it.

That is my Christmas message to you, dear friends and followers.

at the Newport Creamery, are filled with the unknown and, in fact, the unknowable.

Observe "the grace in ordinary life" as Garrison Keillor has said. And be glad you are alive to be a witness to its infinite variety.

For instance, I was struck by the fact that the wife calls him Daddy. That puts a felt, affectionate underpinning to her otherwise blunt words. She shows us a sense of motherliness and personal caring in her intentions toward her husband. "Daddy" had a cozy sound coming from her. Listen to the music that plays along with the words.

He responds with predictable male resistance and furthermore saves his sense of masculine freedom by showing his bright plumage to the favorite waitress who handles the whole messy business with practicality, kindness and humor. We often do these things instinctively and don't realize how truly masterful we are at life.

Many couples I've seen over the years engage in this kind of banter. It becomes second nature, you might notice. Young couples often establish a symbiosis and dependency that pulls them like magnets toward one another and they finish each other's sentences. Call it

and respect with individual difference as they become separate persons in their own right, while still loving each other and caring for each other. That takes a while. And a bit of living.

There is another style of attaching that couples fall into that is quite well known to us. Some couples stay together by fault finding. This involves "communication problems" which sometimes brings a couple to the door of a counselor or therapist. Therapy with this couple usually begins with their wish to not leave the marriage. Each wants the therapist to change the other one, the one who is *wrong*, so they can be happy. While it is true, they have fallen into a pattern of dysfunction, it "works" for them to not examine places of true unhappiness – usually because they don't know how to start. So while they are each lonely inside themselves, they stick together because they would be lost without the other. This is a very workable problem if there is good will and good memories and both are able to laugh at themselves at times.

Of course there are couples that bond through negative attachment as well. These are the George's and Martha's who use and misuse each other and won't part because of deeper fears and secrets. And, yes, they usually scare us to death and we avoid invitations to be with them. Call them unlucky, but there is no doubt, they have found a way to connect and keep going.

What I love about being a writer, the blank page allows me to write things down *in vivo,* that wonderful world where things don't have to make sense. They just are. The richness is in the mystery and in the living, itself.

I thank this couple who made me smile at the Newport Creamery. We are all in this together after all.

Merry Christmas and Happy Holidays, dear friends and followers. Where ever you are is exactly the right place at this moment in time. Savor it. See you in the New Year!

"Wonder Woman" the film, is a heightened portrayal of our deepest human drives to survive and win in battle. Only in this case, the power originates in the land of the Amazons, a tribe of strong women, and tells the tale of the creation and evolution of the child who becomes Wonder Woman.

As she experiences the world outside her Utopian homeland, she must learn to use her warrior skills well. And she does.

As Diana, goddess of the hunt, she is perfectly named. She is the rescuer of the man. She does not fall helplessly in love and subvert her strengths into support, marriage and babies. She even, quite knowingly and deftly, sees and releases the soul of a maimed and captured female chemist for the war known as Dr. Poison.

My own take-away the next morning: every woman needs to connect with her best warrior self at some points in her life.

After the show my friends and I enjoyed a celebratory power beverage and a hearty exchange of ideas along with that special bonding laughter only women understand. We left the restaurant reluctantly when we heard the whirring of the vacuum cleaner and saw the kindly smiles of the wait staff. We hugged each other on the sidewalk and said good night, feeling the power and percolating with the pleasure of the evening.

When I arrived home quite late my ideal husband was waiting up for me.

A Mother's Day Love Letter
My Mother's Hats

This tribute is to Mary Collins, my mother, who taught me about life with her many sorrows and filled me with longing for her unfulfilled dreams. It was Gloria Steinem, however, in her essay entitled, "Ruth's Song Because She Could Not Sing It," who planted in me the life-giving drive to make my mother's life count – for both of us.

It's all I ever wanted

This phrase of longing makes me think of Miss Mary. Miss Mary is what I affection-

to her sometimes, ten years after she left this earth. That's when I say things like, Well Miss Mary, what'd you think of that! A really dirty house. At other moments I say aloud, You would just love this rose garden, Miss Mary, or, real peach ice cream, your favorite! Isn't it funny, Miss Mary, that after a lifetime of eating fresh food, you became so crazy about that popcorn chicken at the Newport Creamery? I remember when you wouldn't "lower yourself," as you used to say, to walk into a place where no one knew how to dress.

Although she was, in fact, my mother, somewhere along the way of caretaking of her, she stopped being my mother and became a very nice elderly lady who loved popcorn chicken in a basket, French fries and a coke.

Miss Mary and my mother had one thing, though, in common. She only wanted to be a Lady. That's all she ever wanted. She would have, indeed, made a better full-time Lady than a mother. After all, who could expect a 5 foot 2 inch, 115 pound-Lady to give birth to twins and then be expected to actually *raise* them, clean house all day and be married to, yes, go ahead and say it, a railroader, of all things. She was meant for a better life. She could have married Roy Dietz from Wrightsville I'll have

stressed, *three*, mind you. Both those men have well-dressed wives, she solemnly explained, who have furs and magnificent jewelry from Riese's Fine Jewelry in downtown York. Wives who never worry about a THING. They just adorn the arm of the man who cares for them. They know how to live, believe you me, she concluded with a declaratory nod of her head.

Many of her declarations had the tendency to nip disagreements in the bud, along with her famous dismissive comment, You Just Don't Understand. That and the frequent times she lay trembling in bed with her sickness precluded any serious attempt at a two way conversation.

If my mother had been honest, even though that was "not done" in her day, I think I would have heard a different story. A deeper story.

I could have been a Lady, she would say, and had a good life, if I hadn't come down with scarlet fever when I was fourteen. All my teeth came loose and were pulled out and I had to get dentures, which hurt. I hated the way I looked. My hair also fell out in big clumps before I finally recovered from the fever. It did grow back, curly too. But then it turned overnight from black to white and by the time I was thirty-five I had all white hair. I missed school

I had to quit school, she would have revealed with sadness, because my mother needed me at home to cook and clean. Your grandfather was sick and Marie, Ralph and Clara were still at home. My mother had a lot on her. I'd always wanted to be in a musical at school, but, goddam, it turned out that all I was good for was cooking and cleaning. I resented that all my life but what would be the point of saying so. No, you didn't know I swear, did you? The nurses told me I swore like a marine under anesthesia when you and Lance were born.

Your Aunt Helen had everything. A beautiful house outside of Philadelphia with a cleaning woman. Your Uncle Matson was a mushroom grower for Campbell's Soup. They knew how to live, believe you me. Even though your Aunt Helen got migraines her entire married life, and jumped out of her skin whenever the phone rang, she had a better life – one that I wish I had. She left home at nineteen to study to be a milliner. Then she met your Uncle Matson and he took her away to Philadelphia.

It was Helen who showed me how to decorate a house, how to carve a roast, set a table, and who told me about Pauline, the milliner in downtown York. So one night after ironing for hours, and your dad was still down

at the train yard doing overtime, I decided I am going to have a hat made. Over the years, Pauline made me about forty-five hats – all from money I saved out of the grocery money. I loved those hats.

When I walked into St. Peter's Lutheran church on Sunday mornings, I thought, I'm going to hold my head high because I know I look smart and elegant in this hat. You would never know what I came from in this hat. No country girl, no outhouse, no leaving school in 9th grade, no scarlet fever, no endless cooking and cleaning, putting laundry through the wringer, ruining my hands, starching and ironing the night away.

They are staring and whispering. They just want to see what hat Mary Collins is wearing this week. Don't

felt asked me to come over for cards next Wednesday. As if I would go to *her* house down there on Duke Street, of all places. As if I care to mingle with Rosemary Hershey who dresses like a prostitute. You might wonder why in the world I took a job packing candy at Wolfgang's Candy Factory with these women. I needed the money – plain and simple. Besides, it turned out that we had a pretty good time at the factory. Even though these women came from run-down neighborhoods and used coarse language, I have to say, they were fun and for those few weeks before Christmas and Easter, I looked forward to getting out of this house. But your Aunt Helen would never understand that.

When I went to the hospital for all those shock treatments, you wouldn't believe the class of people I had to put up with. I don't see how the doctors stand it. Dr. Greenstein said he thought my depression went all the way back to when I was fourteen, but I think it would be gone today if only your dad would buy me a beautiful house.

The doctor liked your dad. He thought he was depressed too. As if I care if he's depressed. I'm the one that's depressed. He wants to know what depressed feels like, just ask me. I'll tell him. I'll tell you one thing,

All I ever wanted was to be a Lady and be admired for my posture, how I set a table, my proper use of language and for my taste in hats. Now tell me, is that asking too much?

Sometimes I wonder if Miss Mary likes the class of people in heaven and I smile. I hope she has found a milliner and I hope, above all, she feels like a Lady up there.

Happy Mother's Day, Miss Mary. I promise to take care of both our dreams and our creative life force. You never got the chance and you deserved it. I'll do my very best to move us both forward with my own song. It's your song too.

Love that goes beyond understanding, Your Daughter.

Do the Right Thing

I was raised in York, Pennsylvania, as a Lutheran, a religion that espouses a doctrine of faith, good works and hopeful receivers of the Grace of God. Oh, and "where all the women are strong, all the men are good-looking, and all the children are above average". – (Garrison- you-know-who)

I just finished reading the following piece in the New York Times and knew I had to respond. I haven't written a Blog in a long while and it is way overdue. Thanks for your patience, hoping you may have missed me, friends and followers!

*https://www.nytimes.com/2017/10/25/us/
senator-jeff-flake-mormon.html*

Laurie Goodstein, reporting on religion in her latest NYT's piece, "Flake's Speech Bore Marks of Mormon Faith as Well as Politics," seeks to bring an academic construction/analysis to bear. In my opinion, Jeff

derlies all faiths. In my own family, we have a variety of religious faiths represented, including the choice of no religion. We are fortunate that we don't go to battle over this, but to the contrary, we respect and love each other.

I certainly took History of Religion when getting my BA at Connecticut College in Philosophy and it did what was intended; it stretched my mind and made me more open to, and accepting of, a variety of ways of looking at divinity and practicing what gets preached in our everyday lives. This, it is assumed, makes us better and helps us do the right thing.

Ergo, all religions aim to do the right thing. Ok, some of them get more fussy about it than others. My opinion again. But there is a difference between discernment and inner peace vs. anger and bitterness.

Next, in taking Sociology and Psychology, I learned that we humans are social beings by nature and become our best in relationship with others, even though we don't always do the right thing. Nevertheless, we have a foundation of security, betterment and inspiration to support us. I also learned in Psychology that we are indeed shaped by the forces and beliefs that we took in by osmosis learning, behavioral reward or punishment,

of belief that lasts a lifetime.

There is nothing "wrong" with being a Mormon and living out one's belief in doing the right thing and seeing the sense for others to be honorable also. And there is nothing "wrong" with being a Lutheran and doing good works and doing the right thing and encouraging others to be honorable. Finally there is nothing "wrong" but rather quite right with being a politician and reminding one's fellow and female cohorts to live out their chosen profession doing the right thing. Thank you, Senator Jeff Flake.

Postscript: I have never written about religion or politics – and maybe I never will again. I would love to hear your comments just the same.

One afternoon in July, three years ago, I got a call from my twin brother. He said, "Sit down. I have something to tell you." But I already knew "something big" was in that message. I was, at the time he called, in the ER, in a hospital bed, getting my vitals checked from a severe attack of panic which came on during a yoga class where I usually felt nothing but calm. Here's the story.

When we were little fishes, happily floating around in my mother's amniotic fluid, we had wordless knowledge of the other. Bumping, reaching, sleeping, looking at one another. Maybe we had telepathy, who knows?

"You ready to be born?"

"No, you?"

"Don't know. They're turning me around to go, not sure I'm going to like this."

life to ponder what this would mean later. I just took it for granted like the wheat fields in Pennsylvania we came to expect, those amber waves of grain, and the spectacular summer lightning storms we admired from Grandmother's windows while Grandma called, "Stay away from the windows."

Native American lore tells of knowing who your parents will be before you are born. You look down from the sky and see your new family. How would that feel?

"I'm scared," said my brother in the warm space we share.

"Don't be scared, Lance. I think we get held a lot by all the aunties, even if mother is sick. Besides, they're only saying she's sick but maybe she isn't."

"I hope she isn't."

"Me too."

Home base and identity are formed in these soundless conversations. This is where we came from; this is what we know. Our rude expulsion into the world of unknowns must come to its natural conclusion. There are suddenly strong, determined contractions.

"Uh oh, here goes," said Lance who would precede me by twelve long minutes.

"Wait!"

that you'll always let me know when you're in trouble and so will I. Cross your heart and hope to die."

"How will I do that?"

"Just think about us and I'll get the message."

"I'm not coming in as a very spiritual person," said Lance, already bringing his wry self front and center..

"Hey!" "No excuses!"

"Ok, ok, I promise."

"Wait!"

"*What*? I can't hold on here."

"Let me hear your heart one more time."

"What for?"

I reached out with my new baby fingers and touched his soft baby hand, bigger than mine, against the membrane that separated us.

"Because then I'll always have it to remember for ever and ever."

"This is a big waste of time, "Lance said, foretelling of our future conversations.

I was undaunted.

"Let me float over to your chest. Move your arm out of the way. There. Yes, I can hear it, Lance! It's the sound of Home! Woosh. Woosh. You want to hear mine?"

"See you later, brother!" I called into the dark. "Don't forget to breathe and yell and tell them there's another one."

Later, on earth, York, Pennsylvania: Twins were born to Mr. and Mrs. Harrell Woodrow Collins. Presiding was Dr. Clyde Seitz. Mother and a son and a daughter are doing well. Father is beside himself. Relatives flock to help.

So began the symbiosis, so common and yet not commonly understood, known to many sets of twins. It's a loyalty beyond words to describe. There's arguing and conflict when asserting autonomy and temperament needs. There's dependency, competition and adventure. There's being alone and there's the perfect rightness of being together. Later, we would cry when we were separated in first grade.

You and me as one yet two. Twins.

Our bond was heightened by being treated as one unit, often in the carriage where we mostly slept. Our bond was also heightened by the struggle to survive a fragile, depressed mother and a proud, gentle father who escaped conflict and a sick wife and sought peace

The resulting solace that occurred between Lance and me is wordless, having taken shape before speech, followed by two silent little kids who didn't know what to say and figured keeping quite was the best thing; perhaps it would help get Mother well. It was a powerful template for our safety together in the world.

Years later, Lance is diagnosed with an incurable form of leukemia. He lives in Indiana and I live in Rhode Island. I visit him a month before he dies. He's angry. How come I was so different from him? How come I put happy pictures up on Facebook? Why did I wear rose-colored glasses? Why did I think life is so great ("when your brother is sick " was left unsaid.)?

"I don't know, Lance. Maybe it was because I had an easy birth because you paved the way for us. And, I *like* the pictures I post. They make me happy." I knew this was about giving his pain and fears a needed voice, so I didn't say that every time I called him, first thing he often said was, "Hey, I'm just headed out the door, I'll call ya later," and that had made me sad. I listened and he talked, in a heart-wrenching way.

dreamer, along with a list of other hard indignities this caused him. Before we left the parking lot at Starbucks, we were both speaking in rather croaky voices. I turned on the ignition and said, "Do you think we opened the door a little bit?" Lance said, "We'll see." I knew that meant we did – a little bit.

The night before he died I couldn't sleep back in Rhode Island. I got up at midnight with the knowledge that Lance needs me. I stood at the back porch window and watched the full moon above the tall pines against the night sky. I sang little songs to Lance, the very same songs I sang when he couldn't sleep when we were six years old as the tears ran down my cheeks.

"It's ok, honey boy"
"I love you, brother."
"I'm right here"
"I'll see you later."

I knew beyond all that's rational that he heard me. At 3:00 a.m. I went back to bed and slept deeply.

The following day I got the call that Lance died. At home. With Hospice care. With love of his wife and step-daughter and grandson's hugs and kisses to see him off to heaven. His wife told me he'd had a more peaceful night than usual.

Questions came pouring into my head in the middle of the night over the next months. Why *did* I see myself as his protector, his guardian angel of sorts? Was I all wrong? Was I blinded? And should I have been more practical? Should I have gone to doctor visits with him instead of letting things run their course while I said prayers and read about leukemia? Perhaps being raised by a seriously depressed mother who believed that World War II meant "the world is not going to last much longer." made its mark on us. It had been a very

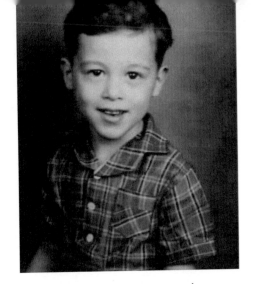

Lance – First Grade

Linda – First Grade

radio and their all-knowing mother's ominous remarks.

But we did not die in the woods like Hansel and Gretel. Lance went on to be a realist and a pharmacist and I went on to be an idealist and a psychotherapist while my brother made tons of friends with his sardonic and brilliant wit, funny but not malicious, that drew people to him.

However, that pull of fate remained powerful in both of us throughout our lives. I strongly feel Lance would have turned down, derided even, my offer of anything spiritual. I feel he would have turned down my suggestions of alternative cancer treatments, possible solutions that made me hopeful and gave me strength.

He was a pharmacist and a believer in what science says is true – with more studies needed. He was a realist and a financial planner and worrier about overspending. Did I let him down? Were my optimistic and idealistic ways of no use to Lance's view of life? In the end, I chose to respect and allow Lance's choices to hold sway and not intrude mine. That struck me as his human right. However, hundreds of moments of deep pain clawed at me during many nights and I was plagued by searing self-doubt.

On my visit to him in Indianapolis the month before he died, after he got all of his anger at me spent, he said, "Tomorrow I want you to drive me to downtown Indianapolis and I want to show you all my favorite places, including the medical center where I go for treatment."

After breakfast, we drove to see the place where Robert F. Kennedy had given a speech, the steps where President Bill Clinton had delivered a message, the Kurt Vonnegut Library, the college where his step-daughter was going to teach. Then Lance said, "I want to be buried in a place that is quiet and near a University. Let's drive to the Butler area. It's nice there and young couples settle there."

We went on a small excursion to try out the feel of his final resting place to see if it suited him. It was January, cold and grey and brown. However, the grounds were well cared for and Lance liked it. I was struck by the sadness and yet closeness of what he was sharing with me. He was with me in the beginning and he wanted to show me where he would be at the end.

At his funeral, I would place a copy of Jack London's "The Sea Wolf" near his hand so he'd have something good to read. As I touched that hand I thought this is the

Later, I was invited to select a book from his library. I found a well-worn copy of e. e. cummings with turned down pages here and there. It magically fell open to page 92 in my hands. There underlined in pen, along with a yellowed book mark of pressed field flowers, now brown, and a worn down tassel, I found my brother's heart beat again and I knew, somehow, I would get through this.

"here is the deepest secret nobody knows
(here is the root of the root and the bud of the bud
and the sky of the sky of a tree called life; which grows
higher than the soul can hope or mind can hide)
and this is the wonder that's keeping the stars apart
i carry your heart (i carry it in my heart)"

– e. e. cummings, 95 Poems

What is This Thing Called Love

"And that's all there is to it," as my Grandma Longe would declare at the end of her important sentences.

Whether she was picking a hen to roast for dinner from the tidy chicken shed with warm lamps for the little yellow peeps in the corner, or drying out feathers for the home-made bed pillows for family and for boarders in her spic and span house in the countryside of East Prospect, nursing my grandfather during a long sickness that took his life too early, or getting a Practical Nursing degree in her 60th year and riding the bus to the city several days a week to help with new born babies, or recoveries from surgery, making Sunday dinners for her family who had upgraded their locations to the suburbs, she astonished me. I loved the country life, the homemade quilts and the smell of molasses cookies. I

ing the walkway. It was my summer vacation. I looked up at the cloud formations and had thoughts that now seemed to have understanding beyond my child years.

I've inherited, I'm sure, my love of my work and love of my life from Grandma Longe. I wanted to make things better also like she did.

My work informs my life and my life informs my work. And that's all there is to it.

When I stop to think about all the beautiful souls I've sat with over a period of forty years, actually a drop of time in the ocean of our lives, it has become a treasured collection of magical moments. They live in these walls long after their tourists have returned home. Some of my funnier clients, as in good-humored, have given me the credit, calling me "Glinda".

But the truth is this interior knowledge that brings illumination to their lives has been waiting there all the time for that magical moment when it dawns.

Not that all our lives, yours and mine, aren't full of complexities! Just be a fly on the wall for any session and you'll see those complexities in full colors, many in the darker hues. But there are the moments of clarity, lightness of being and inhaling of one's own breath

– the life force that is always waiting there – that are simply magical in their appearance. An enlivening, an awakening, an acceptance, a new window appears and nothing is the same after that.

Carl Jung, Swiss psychologist, used to say, It's as though you thought you lived all your life in a house that only had one view, that of the river to the east and one day you look and you see a new window to the west that has a view of the mountains. Once that occurs, you can never *not* see the fuller view, whether you wanted to or not, and it changes the way you live your life forever.

atry, located in a clinical setting of community service in New Haven, was a family in distress. All clients were of meager means to seek help. I was plunged, clinically speaking, into deep waters of traumatic experiences but had superior supervision and learned to stay grounded from shocks and to understand that there but for the grace of God could go anyone of us.

The academic year passed and my field placement was over and I accepted a dinner invitation from my first family. It was their gracious thank you. They had stayed solidly in family therapy throughout my placement there and were receiving ongoing services in the community by the time I had to leave. I felt humbled by knowing them and their sincere desire to learn new ways to heal.

Today, my work and my education have taken me through many paths of learning. While I don't see families with such severe issues anymore, I will never forget my first family clients and my respect for the enormous work done in mental health clinics.

There is magic in practical help and there is magic in inner growth work. Both create a bond between me and the clients that have come my way, to find their way.

of love and laughter, tears and bravery, fresh starts, finding peace and those magical moments. May life bring joy to you all. May life's journey be exactly what you need and longed for.

"And that's all there is to it."

But meantime let me go my way
And meantime let me have my say

Your words are true
But mine are too
So let's don't cause our bond to fray.

I won't deny, born glad was I
And you were born the sad one.
As I grow old and I am told
That life must now betray me
I'll never buy it.
It's just a riot

This life of mine has been a wonder
So, truth be told between us,
I'll gladly go up yonder.

And give you yet another chance
To live and learn
The happy dance,
If only I could have the chance.

—*LCT*

Made in the USA
Middletown, DE
06 September 2024

60461266R00044